Tu Youyou

Published in the United States of America by Cherry Lake Publishing
Ann Arbor, Michigan
www.cherrylakepublishing.com

Content Adviser: Jessica Criales, Doctoral Candidate, History Department, Rutgers University
Reading Adviser: Marla Conn MS, Ed., Literacy specialist, Read-Ability, Inc.
Book Design: Jennifer Wahi
Illustrator: Jeff Bane

Photo Credits: ©Bambara/Shutterstock, 5; ©Mr.Suchat/Shutterstock, 7; ©Marilyn barbone/Shutterstock, 9; YamabikaY/Shutterstock, 11; ©Manfred Ruckszio/Shutterstock, 13, 22; ©alexkich/Shutterstock, 15; ©Xinhua / Alamy Stock Photo, 17, 21, 23; ©CC4.0 Bengt Nyman, 19; Cover, 8, 12, 14, Jeff Bane; Various frames throughout, ©Shutterstock Images

Library of Congress Cataloging-in-Publication Data

Names: Spiller, Sara, author. | Bane, Jeff, 1957- illustrator.
Title: Tu Youyou / Sara Spiller [author] ; Jeff Bane [illustrator]
Description: Ann Arbor : Cherry Lake Publishing, 2018. | Series: My
   itty-bitty bio | Includes bibliographical references and index.
Identifiers: LCCN 2018003109| ISBN 9781534128828 (hardcover) | ISBN
   9781534130524 (pdf) | ISBN 9781534132023 (pbk.) | ISBN 9781534133723
   (hosted ebook)
Subjects: LCSH: Pharmacologists--China--Biography--Juvenile literature. |
   Medical scientists--China--Biography--Juvenile literature.
Classification: LCC RS73.T83 S65 2018 | DDC 615.1092 [B] --dc23
LC record available at https://lccn.loc.gov/2018003109

Printed in the United States of America
Corporate Graphics

About the author: Sara Spiller is a native of the state of Michigan. She enjoys reading comic books and hanging out with her cats. She wants to help empower people all over the world, including women engineers.

About the illustrator: Jeff Bane and his two business partners own a studio along the American River in Folsom, California, home of the 1849 Gold Rush. When Jeff's not sketching or illustrating for clients, he's either swimming or kayaking in the river to relax.

I was born in China in 1930.
I grew up with four brothers.

I was sick when I was 16 years old.

This **inspired** me to **cure** others.

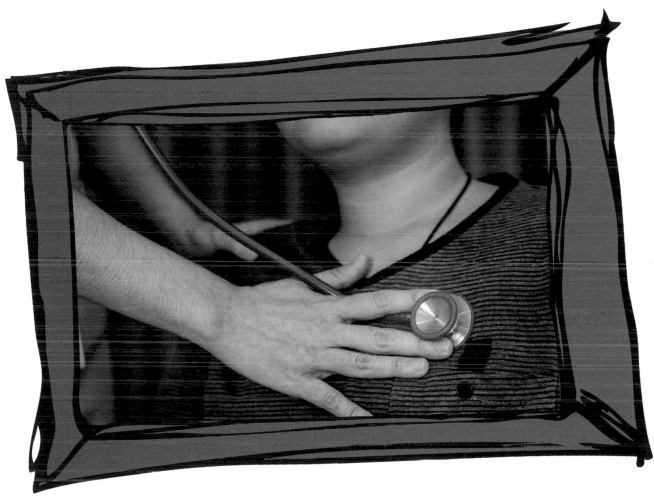

What inspires you?

I went to **pharmacology** school in the city of Beijing.

I studied old Chinese **medicine**.

My country's leader wanted to cure **malaria**. He wanted me to help.

I led a team to stop malaria. It was called Project 523.

What makes a good leader?

I learned about sick people that had malaria. I read **ancient** books.

Sweet wormwood was used in China long ago. I made a medicine out of it.

13

I tested the medicine on myself first. I wanted to be sure it was safe. It worked!

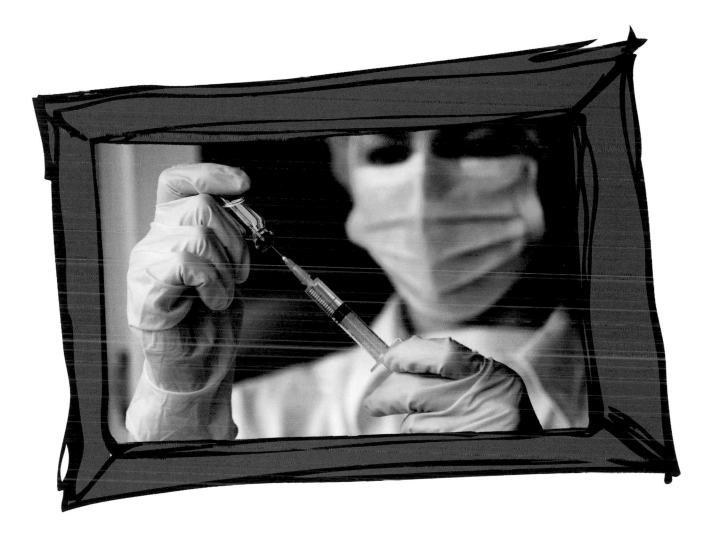

I became the first Chinese woman to win a Nobel Prize.

The award goes to people who do important work. This was in 2015.

Some say I'm **stubborn**. I don't give up.

I work hard. I save lives.

What are your strengths?

I helped the world. Women are smart.

Women can save lives!

What would you like to ask me?

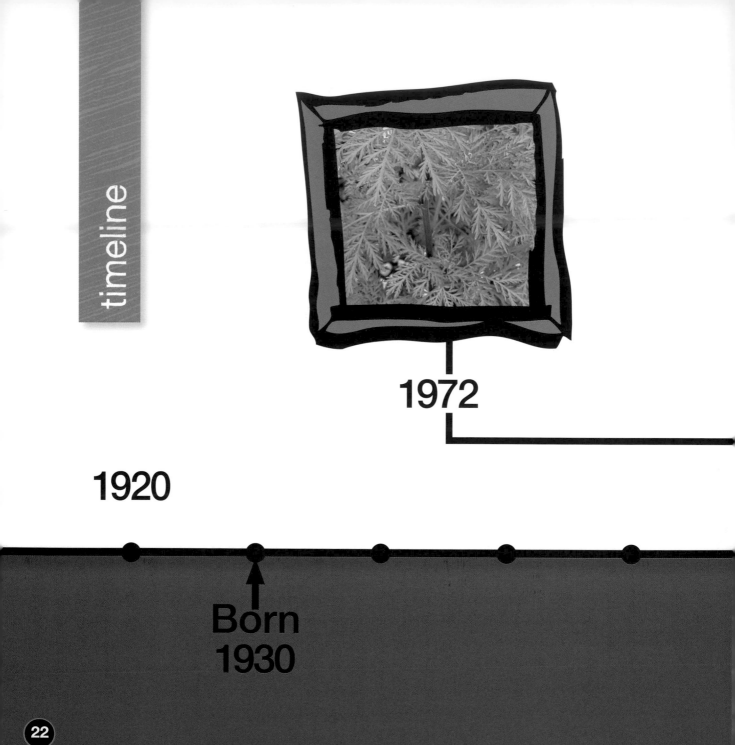

1972

1920

Born
1930

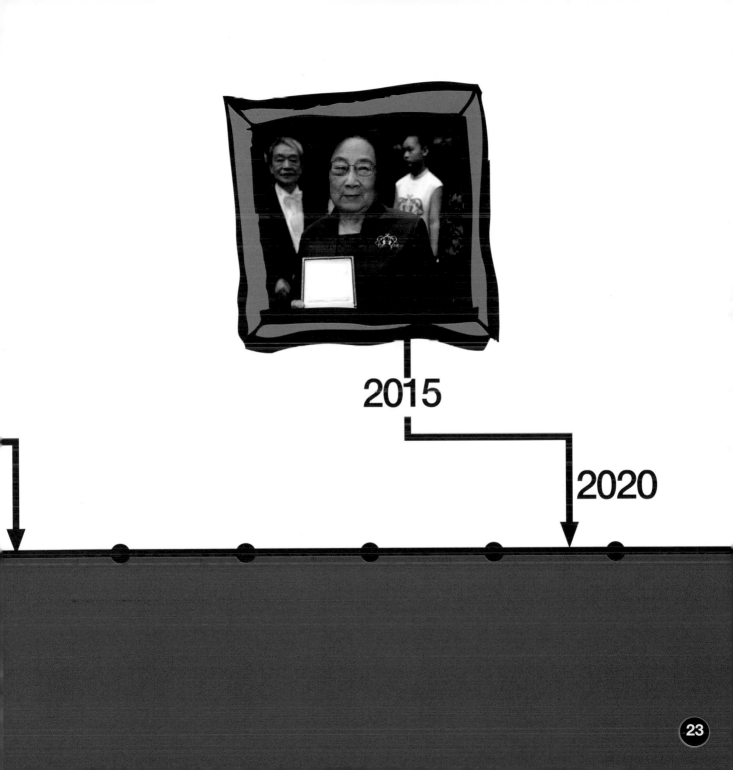

2015

2020

glossary

ancient (AYN-shuhnt) very old

cure (KYOOR) make someone who is sick better

inspired (in-SPYRD) filled someone with a feeling or an idea

malaria (muh-LAIR-ee-uh) a serious illness people get from a kind of mosquito

medicine (MED-ih-sin) something used to treat an illness

pharmacology (phar-muh-KAH-luh-jee) the study of the uses and effects of drugs

stubborn (STUHB-urn) not willing to give in or change

sweet wormwood (SWEET WURM-wud) a plant used for medicine or cooking

index